Sam's Secret

Written by: **Stephanie Comella**

Illustrated by: **Len Gatdula**

An Original Playbook®

presented in....
Playbook® Advantage ✓+ Format

© 2001 Playbooks, Laguna Hills, CA, ALL RIGHTS RESERVED.

GLC K-3
RS 1-3
Story Length: 1,836 Words

Sam's Secret

PUBLISHED BY PLAYBOOKS, INC.
d.b.a. Playbooks Reader's Theater

Copyright © 2001 by Playbooks, Inc., Laguna Hills, CA.
All Rights Reserved.

Playbook, Playbooks, Playbook Format, Roleplay Reader,
Playberized, StageBooks, and Being a Start Makes Reading Fun
are trademarks of Playbooks, Inc.

ISBN 978-1-60476-101-6

The unique format of a Playbook® with character colorization and specialized readability levels is a proprietary method of book structure, writing, format, construction, re-construction, displaying and printing protected under U.S. Patent Nos. 6,683,611, 6,859,206, and 7,456,834 with additional patents pending. For information regarding licensing the rights to write, edit, construct, re-construct, display, print or publish any book in Playbook® format call 1-800-375-2926. No part of this publication may be reproduced in whole or in part, or stored in a retrieval system, or transmitted in any form or by any means, electronic, mechanical, photocopying, recording, or otherwise, without written permission of the publisher, except by a reviewer, who may quote brief passages in a review. For information regarding permission, call Playbooks, Inc. at 1-800-375-2926. This book is subject to the condition that it shall not, by way of trade or otherwise, be re-sold, hired out, or otherwise circulated without the publisher's prior consent in any form of binding or cover other than that in which it is published and without a similar condition including this condition being imposed on the subsequent purchaser. *Performances of this story/script may be videotaped for school or library purposes.*

Being a Star Makes Reading Fun™

Welcome to the world of Playbooks® and the beginning of a wonderful role-play reading adventure! Playbook® stories are presented in a unique and colorful format and are read out loud by several readers like a play, without memorization, props, or a stage. When you read a Playbook®, you and other readers bring the story to life and become the characters. As you read **your** part out loud, you will have fun expressing and acting like your character. You and the other readers will explore the story plot together and learn what will happen next. It's an exciting journey of discovery that pulls you into the story, and you'll want to read it out loud again and again!

HOW TO GET STARTED

Begin your reading adventure with the **Character Summary** here at the beginning of the book. **You'll notice right away that the words and sentences for each character appear in a different color here and throughout the book. This will make it easy to follow along and read your part with confidence and enthusiasm.**

It doesn't matter whether you are a beginning reader or an experienced reader; there is a part for everyone. The number of characters in the story may not match the number of readers in your group and that's okay. Readers can play more than one character role, or readers can share a role by taking turns.

Once your role has been assigned, you and the other readers will each read his or her character's summary out loud from his or her own copy of the book. The most experienced reader typically reads the narrator's role. **It's important for teachers and parents to refer to the Teacher or Parent Guide when assigning roles.**

Have fun bringing your character to life by bringing your voice up and down, speaking softly or loudly, changing your facial expressions, and moving your hands or body. Trying different voices or accents can also be lots of fun.

Sometimes you will see *black italicized text* inside parenthesis before or in the middle of sentences. **These are called "cues" and tell you how to read a sentence with expression.** For example, if the "cue" says *(with surprise),* speak the sentence with surprise in your voice! Cues are not read out loud.

MAKING THE MOST OF THE STORY

It's more fun to read the story out loud together with other readers the first time you read your role. It's exciting to discover the story in this way rather than each reader practicing his or her part alone first. As you get better with your role, you may want to change the way you express your character's personality, or you may want to switch roles with another reader. Be creative! When all your readers get comfortable with their roles, you may want to read the story in front of a friendly audience.

Reading out loud is so much fun that it's easy to forget about the other readers. **So be sure to read with good manners!** Here are some helpful hints. Stay quiet when other readers are reading. Follow along and keep up and be ready to read when it's your turn. Speak loudly and clearly so everyone can hear you. Stay in character for the whole story! Most importantly, enjoy your role-play reading experience. **You and your cast of characters are ready to begin your Playbook® adventure!**

FOR TEACHERS AND PARENTS

For specific guidance on implementing a Playbook® story in the classroom or in the home, download a FREE Teacher or Parent Guide at the following link.
http://www.readerstheater.com/teacherguide.pdf

It's important for students to be assigned a role they can read with success in front of their peers. A "Recommended Reader Assignment" chart that identifies the reading level for each story character is included in this story's group set. To print additional copies, visit www.readerstheater.com/rra.html **and locate the story's title.**

Being an active participant in a story spikes the reader's curiosity to learn more about the story's theme. Rewarding a child for exceptional effort and performance is an excellent practice for boosting a child's reading confidence. To download **FREE Award Certificates** to recognize star performers, visit www.readerstheater.com/awardcertificates.pdf.

Playbooks, Inc. also provides story-specific activity suggestions and worksheets to reinforce concepts and go beyond the story into the content areas of Language Arts, Math, Science, Social Studies, Art, Health, etc., as well as Character Development. Activities range in skill level and age-appropriateness, so the teacher or parent can choose activities that best suit the readers. Activities include comprehension quizzes, crossword puzzles, word search, vocabulary, discussion and writing prompts, story mapping, word problems, etc. To download FREE supplemental activity sheets for this and other stories, visit www.readerstheater.com/supplements.html.

Seeing children develop a passion for reading while working with the Playbook® format will be one of your greatest rewards.

Character Summary

Before beginning this story, it is helpful for each reader to read his/her character's summary aloud.

Tom
I am Tom. I am 4. I like jets. My dog is Sam. I love him.

Sam
I am Tom's best friend. I am still a puppy, and I like to run on the beach. I have a secret. Do you want to know what it is?

Mom
The beach is my favorite place to be on the weekend. I like to rest, read books, and lie in the sun. Doesn't that sound like fun?

Narrator
I must read everything with expression and excitement!

Mom	It's such a nice day outside, Tom. Let's take the dog and go to the beach.
Narrator	Sam, the dog, heard the word "beach" and immediately began running around the house, wagging his tail.
Sam	Ruff-ruff! Did she say the dog is going to the beach? Oh, boy, I think she did! Ruff-ruff!
Tom	Yes, Sam, you can go too.
Narrator	Tom patted Sam on his big fluffy head.

Mom	We can even take a picnic lunch. Tom, you will need a hat to protect your face from the sun.
Tom	Yes, Mom.
Narrator	Mom began to search for Tom's blue sun hat. It was Tom's favorite because it had airplanes on it.
Sam	Ruff-ruff! It looks like Tom has lost his best hat. I know, maybe I can help him find it.
Narrator	Sam went right to Tom's room to look for the hat. He looked under the rug. He looked in the toy box. He finally looked under the bed.

Sam	Ruff-ruff! Here is your hat! I found it! See, I knew I could help!
Mom	Look, Tom. Sam found your hat.
Tom	Sam has my hat! Good boy, Sam!
Mom	All right then, let's go to the beach! Sam Ruff! I want to go now! Ruff-ruff!
Narrator	They quickly arrived at the beach, and Sam couldn't wait to get out of the car.
Sam	Ruff! I want to make sand houses. Can we dig in the sand now?

Tom	Can we dig, Mom?
Mom	First, let's find a good place to sit.
Tom	O.K.
Mom	If we make a sandcastle too close to the water, it could wash away before we're done.
Sam	Ruff! This looks very good. I want to sit here. Ruff-ruff! This is a good place for a dog to sit.
Tom	Sam likes this spot. Sit, boy, sit.
Narrator	Tom pointed his finger at Sam and watched him sit down immediately.

Mom	What a good boy, Sam. Are you ready to build a big sandcastle, Tom?
Sam	Ruff-ruff! I love to play in the sand. I like to make big sand houses.
Tom	Yes, it will be big!
Mom	That's good, Tom. Let's make it strong, too. Go get started!
Sam	Ruff! Yes, dig, dig, dig. Ruff-ruff! We have a big house to make!
Narrator	Tom set his pail down, and Sam eagerly began doing what dogs do best ... dig!
Tom	Wow, Sam, you can dig! Good dog!

Sam	Ruff! This is fun. Ruff-ruff! I love to play in the sand. I even like wet sand!
Mom	Here, Tom. I can do it, too. I'll scoop the sand with my hands.
	If this is going to be the biggest sandcastle on the beach, you're going to need my help.
Tom	Yes, Mom. Help us dig!
Sam	Ruff-ruff! I like to dig at the beach. They let me dig here, but they will not let me dig in Mom's garden.
Narrator	They worked quickly, and soon their sandcastle was taller than Tom!

Mom	Look how tall it stands! Good work, boys. Sam, you're quite the little digger.
Tom	Yes, you are a good digger, Sam!
Narrator	Sam was not paying attention to anything Mom or Tom had said. He spotted a seagull down the beach and was carefully watching every move it made.
Sam	Ruff-ruff! Oh boy, look at that bird. I will have to keep him away from our sand house because birds love sand. Grrrrr!

Narrator	Sam took one big leap toward the seagull.
Mom	Oh, no! Sam, don't jump there!
Tom	No, Sam! Stop!
Mom	Stop, Sam! Stop!
Narrator	Instead of jumping over the sandcastle, Sam landed right on top! The walls crumbled beneath him.
Sam	Ruff! Oh, no! Did I do that? Ruff-ruff!
Narrator	Tom began to cry.
Mom	It's O.K., Tom! Don't be sad. We can build another castle. There's enough sand to build sandcastles all day long.
Narrator	Mom and Tom walked toward their beach blanket. Sam followed close behind and licked one of Tom's hands.
Tom	I am sad. I am very sad!

Sam	Ruff-ruff! I am very sorry, Tom. But do not worry. I will fix the sand house. Ruff-ruff! I will make a bigger one. You will see. Please do not be sad, Tom.
Mom	Sam, why don't you go chase birds for a while? Go on now. Tom would like to rest a bit.
	Don't worry, Tom. We have all day to play on the beach. After lunch, we can start over.
Narrator	Suddenly, they heard Sam barking frantically. They both turned to see an amazing sight!

Mom	Look, Tom! The sandcastle is fixed. It's even taller than the first one! How on earth did Sam do that by himself?
Tom	Wow! Sam is the very best dog. I am not sad now.
Sam	Ruff-ruff!
Tom	Look, Mom, Sam is hot. Can we go in now?
Mom	I think we should eat lunch first. Is anyone hungry? Let's see what's in the basket.
Sam	Ruff-ruff! Did I hear the word "lunch"? Oh boy! I am hungry!

Mom	What do you want to eat, Tom?
Narrator	Tom jumped up and down.
Tom	I want a hot dog.
Mom	That sounds good to me. Let's race to the hot dogs!
Sam	Ruff! On your mark ... get set ... ruff!
Tom	1 ... 2 ... 3 ... go!
Narrator	Off they ran. Tom reached the blanket first, followed by Sam, who began to smother him with big, wet doggy kisses.
Tom	I win, Sam!

Narrator	Tom gobbled up his hot dog, and Mom gave Sam a bone, which made him just as happy.
Mom	You may go swimming, Tom, after you rest awhile. You don't want to get a stomach ache by swimming too soon after you eat.
Tom	O.K., Mom!
Sam	Ruff! I want to play with the Frisbee®. Ruff-ruff!
Mom	Look, Tom. Sam dropped the Frisbee® at your feet. He wants to play! Throw it and see if he can get it.

Tom	Go get it, boy!
Narrator	Tom picked up the Frisbee® and threw it toward the water. Sam soared through the air.
Mom	Nice catch, Sam. Did you see how high he jumped? You'd think he had wings!
Tom	Yes. Good job, Sam!
Sam	Ruff! Throw it again. Watch how high I can go this time! Ruff-ruff!
Narrator	Sam then dropped the Frisbee® at Tom's feet and waited for Tom to throw it again.
Tom	Sit, Sam. Good boy.
Mom	What a good dog he is. Throw the Frisbee® for him again.
Narrator	Just as Sam jumped up, a seagull snatched the Frisbee® out of the air.
Sam	Ruff-ruff! It is that bird again. He has been a problem all day.

Mom	Poor Sam. Maybe he'll find his Frisbee® later. Let's look for his ball in the beach bag.
Tom	Mom, I do not see the ball in the bag.
Narrator	Suddenly, Sam saw the seagull swoop down out of the sky. He flew right toward them with the Frisbee® still in his claws!
Sam	Ruff-ruff! There is that bird again! Now I can get my Frisbee® back! Oh, no, the bird is going to drop it on Mom! Ruff-ruff!

Narrator	Sam jumped up into the air and grabbed the Frisbee® just seconds before it would have landed on Mom's head. He then tumbled into the sand and let out a big yelp. Mom and Tom turned quickly.
Mom	Sam, are you all right? How did you get the Frisbee® from that bird?
Tom	Good boy, Sam! You got it!
Mom	What a good dog, Sam. You are amazing!
Narrator	Sam proudly held the Frisbee® in his mouth.

Tom	Sam is hot, Mom.
Sam	Ruff! Yes, I want to swim in the cool water. Ruff!
Tom	Can we go in?
Mom	Sam sure looks ready for a swim. O.K., go ahead, but be careful!
Tom	Yes, Mom, we will.
Sam	Ruff! I love swimming in the cool water! Come on, Tom! Ruff-ruff!
Narrator	Tom took two small steps toward the ocean just as a wave crashed to shore and splashed him.

Sam	Ruff! Watch this, Tom. I can surf the waves. Ruff!
Mom	Wow, look at that! Sam looks like he's bodysurfing. Do you want to try it with me, Tom? You just swim on top of the wave.
Tom	I don't know.
Mom	I'll hold your hand, and we'll stay in the little waves close to the shore.
Tom	O.K., but how do I get on top of it?
Mom	The wave just comes in and picks you up. Give me your hand, and we can try together.
Tom	1... 2 ... 3 ... go!

Mom	Hold on, Tom. Here comes a wave now!
Tom	Do not let go of me, Mom.
Sam	Ruff! Be careful, Tom. Do not let go of your Mom's hand. Ruff-ruff.
Narrator	Mom kept a sturdy hold on Tom's hand while they rode on top of the wave.
Mom	Wasn't that fun?
Tom	Yes, that was fun!
Sam	Ruff! Come on, Tom. Do it again. We will all do it together this time. Ruff-ruff!

Mom	Sam loves to surf. Let's try it again with him.
Tom	Yes, Sam can do it.
Narrator	The next wave came in too quickly, and it knocked Tom over before he could grab his mother's hand.
Mom	Tom, it's O.K. Just stand up! The water is shallow.
Narrator	Sam couldn't see Tom, so he got nervous. He began to bark frantically and then dove into the water.
Sam	TOM! TOM! Ruff-ruff!
Narrator	Sam saw Tom's feet under the water and grabbed him by the back of the shorts. He dragged him up the sandy shore.
Mom	Tom! Are you all right?
Tom	Yes, Mom. I am O.K. I was on top. Did you see me?
Mom	Yes, I could see you. You're a very good swimmer! Sam is a great swimmer, too.
Tom	Yes, he helped me.

Mom	He loves you, Tom. There's no doubt about that.
Tom	I love him, too.
Mom	Sam is tired now, and he has gone to lie down. I think it's time to go home.
Sam	Ruff! I am tired, Ruff-ruff. Let's go home!
Tom	I want to go, too. I dug in the sand. I got wet. I had fun, and Sam did, too.
Mom	Yes, Tom, we had many adventures today.
Tom	It was fun!
Mom	I still don't know how Sam fixed the castle or got the Frisbee® back.
Tom	Sam is a very good dog. I am happy he is my dog.
Mom	I don't know how he pulled you out of the ocean either. That dog has some pretty amazing secrets! I guess we'll never know. Sam is our little "angel."

Narrator	What Mom and Tom don't know is that Sam really is an angel. Their day at the beach was perfect ... thanks to Sam, the little "angel" sent from above.
Sam	Ruff-ruff! I can keep a secret, can you?

THE END

www.ingramcontent.com/pod-product-compliance
Lightning Source LLC
Chambersburg PA
CBHW050048080526
44586CB00014B/1512